At Home with Science

Colour and Noise!

Let's play with toys

Written by Janice Lobb

Illustrated by Peter Utton and Ann Savage

KING*f*ISHER

KINGFISHER
Kingfisher Publications Plc
New Penderel House
283-288 High Holborn
London WC1V 7HZ
www.kingfisherpub.com

First published by Kingfisher Publications Plc 2001
10 9 8 7 6 5 4 3 2 1

1TR/0501/FR/SC/128JDA

Created and designed by Snapdragon Publishing Ltd
Copyright © Snapdragon Publishing Ltd 2001

A CIP catalogue record for this book is available
from the British Library.

ISBN 0 7534 0560 1

Printed in Hong Kong/China

Author Janice Lobb
Illustrators Peter Utton and Ann Savage

For Snapdragon
Editorial Director Jackie Fortey
Art Director Chris Legee
Designers Chris Legee and Joy Fitzsimons

For Kingfisher
Editors Jennie Morris and Emma Wild
Series Art Editor Mike Davis
DTP Manager Nicky Studdart
Production Debbie Otter

Contents

About this book

Y ou may think that making music, creating your own masterpiece with paints, or riding a bike has nothing to do with science – but it does! This book shows you how to make exciting discoveries while you are playing with your toys.

What if?

Which?

Where?

Why?

How?

Hall of Fame

Archie and his friends are here to help you. They are each named after a famous scientist – apart from Bob the duck, who is a young scientist just like you!

Archie

ARCHIMEDES (287–212BC) The Greek scientist Archimedes worked out why things float or sink while in the bath. According to the story, he was so pleased that he leapt out, shouting 'Eureka!' which means 'I've done it!'

Frank

BENJAMIN FRANKLIN (1706–1790) This American statesman carried out a famous (but dangerous) experiment in 1752. By flying a kite in a storm, he proved that a flash of lightning was electricity. This helped people to protect buildings during storms.

Marie

MARIE CURIE (1867–1934) Girls did not go to university in Poland, where Marie Curie grew up, so she went to study in Paris, France. She worked on radioactivity and received two Nobel prizes for her discoveries, in 1903 and 1911.

Dot

DOROTHY HODGKIN (1910–1994) Dorothy Hodgkin was a British scientist who made many important discoveries about molecules and atoms, the tiny particles that make up everything around us. She was given the Nobel prize for Chemistry in 1964.

See for yourself!

1 Read about the science in your playroom, then try the 'See for yourself!' experiments to discover how it works. In science, experiments try to find or show the answers.

2 Read the instructions for each experiment carefully, making sure you follow the numbered steps in the correct order.

3 Here are some of the things you will need. Have everything ready before you start each experiment.

Mirrors

Cereal box

Salt

Matchboxes

Magnet

Building blocks

Bowl

Flour

Plastic tub

Coin

Cotton reels

Wool

Card

Scissors

Tape

Paper clip

Beads

Buttons

Shoelaces

Colouring pencils

4 # Safety first!

Some scientists took risks to make their discoveries, but our experiments are safe. Just make sure that you tell an adult what you are doing, and get their help when you see the red warning button.

Amazing facts

WOW!

You'll notice that some words are written in *italics*. You can learn more about them from the glossary at the back of the book. And if you want to find out some amazing facts, look out for the 'Wow!' panels.

Look out for the useful tips!

Have fun!

5

What are toys made of?

Children have played with toys for thousands of years. In the past, people made toys from any materials they could find. They were sewn from stuffed rags, *moulded* from clay, carved in bone or wood, plaited from straw, or made of metals like tin or lead. Some of these materials were not always safe for children to play with. Today, shops are full of toys that are bright, colourful and safe to use. Many are still made from cloth, metal and wood, but most toys are *mass-produced* in cheap, modern materials, such as *plastic*.

What happened to the wooden car?

It wooden go!

Toy factory

In a factory, large numbers of toys can be made at once. When plastic is heated, it becomes soft and can be moulded into any shape or size. When plastic cools down, it hardens, and keeps the shape of the mould.

Mould

Red-hot metal is poured into a hole in the mould.

Mould

Moulded toy duck

Like plastic, metal also goes runny when it is very hot, and can be poured into moulds to make toys. When it has cooled down, it can be painted.

See for yourself!

1 Which of your toys are soft? Sort out those toys that are made of materials like rubber or cloth.

Rag doll

Rubber ball

Cloth teddy bear

2 Now sort out your metal toys. Metal is easy to spot because it is usually hard, cold and shiny.

Car

Lorry

Plane

3 Are any of your toys made of natural materials? Wood, cardboard, rope and cloth come from plants.

Cardboard jigsaw puzzle

Wood

Skipping rope

Felt puppet

Rope

4 Most of your toys are probably made from man-made materials, like plastic. How many different shapes and colours can you find? Are the plastic toys hard or soft?

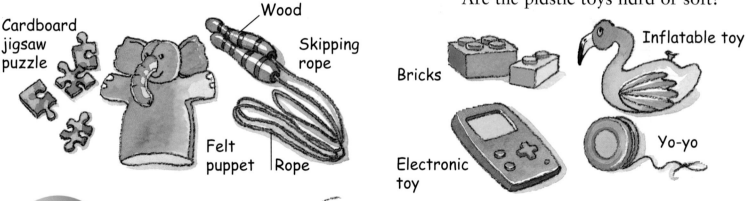

Bricks

Inflatable toy

Electronic toy

Yo-yo

WOW!

Boneshakers!

Bicycles weren't always as comfortable as they are today. This model from 1870 had wooden wheels. It was called a boneshaker because it gave people a very bumpy ride!

Look out for the safety symbol!!

What's in my paint-box?

What bow can't be untied?

A rainbow!

Each paint in your paint-box gets its colour from a substance called a *pigment*. In daylight, we are able to see a pigment's true colour. The Sun's white light is a mixture of coloured lights, which we can see when they are separated out in a rainbow. When sunlight falls on a pigment, some of the light is taken in, or *absorbed*. The colour we see depends on what light is bounced off, or *reflected*, back to our eyes. For example, we say a pigment is green if it reflects green light and absorbs all other colours.

Seeing colours

Yellow, red and blue are the three *primary colours*. You can make other colours by mixing them together.

A pigment which absorbs all the light falling on it, and does not reflect any back, looks black.

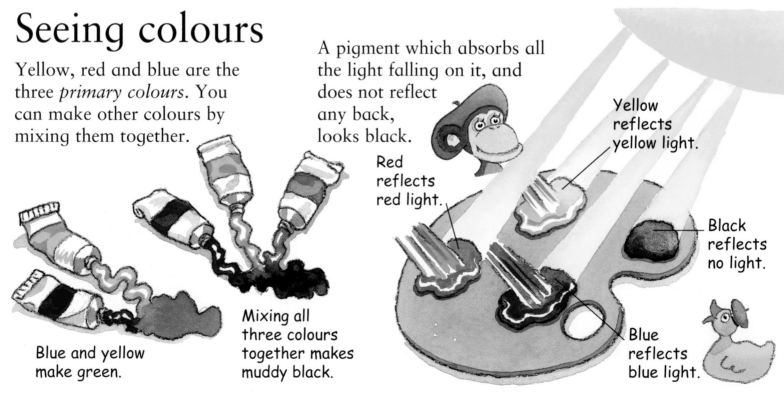

Blue and yellow make green.

Mixing all three colours together makes muddy black.

Red reflects red light.

Yellow reflects yellow light.

Black reflects no light.

Blue reflects blue light.

See for yourself!

1 Divide a circle of white card into three segments with a pencil and colour them red, yellow and blue – the primary colours.

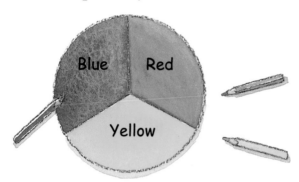

2 Thread wool, or string, through two small holes in the centre of the circle. Use a button to protect the holes.

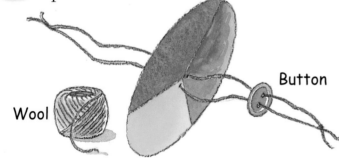

Wool

Button

3 Swing the disc round to twist the wool, then pull the ends tight to make it spin. The colours go round so fast, your eyes can't keep up and the card looks grey!

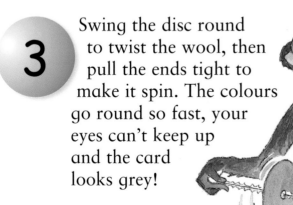

Prehistoric paint!

WOW!

Today, most of the pigments we use are man-made chemicals, but some natural colours have been used for thousands of years. Prehistoric people made drawings of animals on cave walls using chalk and burnt sticks and painted them with coloured earth and ground-up rocks.

Remember to look after your brushes!

How do things stay up?

What did one wall say to the other?

Meet you at the corner!

You wouldn't expect people to use soft materials to make buildings. Buildings have to be made from materials that are not easily stretched, pulled or squashed out of shape. They also have to be strong, so they do not break easily. Wooden building blocks are stiff and strong. If you stand them on the floor, any *force* you put on them goes through them to the floor without making them change shape. But blocks made from foam rubber aren't as stiff, and squash when you push them.

Forces

Even a tall stack of blocks stays firm if the force pushing down on it is *vertical*. The tower doesn't topple over, and the blocks don't move, because the floor pushes back.

Vertical force

Floor pushes back ↑

If the force on a stack of bricks is not vertical, it will fall sideways. Bricks stay up better if they are fixed to another wall and if they are joined together.

One wall supports the other.

The stiff walls and base of this doll's-house help each other stay standing up.

See for yourself!

1 Gently bend a piece of card to form an arch. Will it stand up? The ends try to spread out and flatten the card.

2 Try to support the arch with building blocks. See how many blocks you have to put at each end to keep it arched.

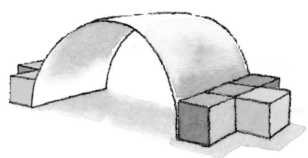

3 Rest some card across the top of the arch, and support its ends. Stand a tin of food in the middle.

The tin's weight pushes the sides of the arch, not the middle.

4 Try to build the bridge again without the arch. The weight of the tin will make the bridge collapse in the middle.

Thinking big!

WOW!

Tiny plastic bricks can be fitted together to make very large structures. Some theme parks contain model villages, towns and whole landscapes made from thousands of toy bricks.

Remember to put your blocks away!

Why do towers topple?

All over the Earth, there is an invisible force called *gravity* that pulls everything down to the ground. The effect of gravity is strongest in the middle of an object, at a spot called its *centre of gravity*. When you put a block on top of a tower, gravity will not pull it off if there are enough blocks under its centre of gravity to support it. If you push the tower over, you remove that support, and the tower topples.

What's tall, thin and wobbly?

The Trifle Tower!

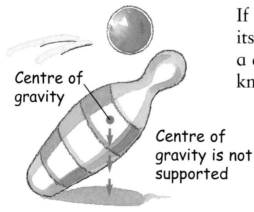

Centre of gravity

A tall, thin object, such as a skittle, is easy to knock over. We say it is *unstable*. The smaller its base, the more unstable an object is.

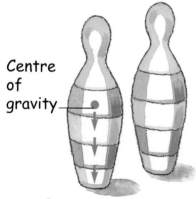

Centre of gravity

Base is under centre of gravity

Centre of gravity

Centre of gravity is not supported

A skittle falls over if you hit it with a ball, because its centre of gravity is no longer over its base.

If you stand a domino on its end, it is unstable. In a domino rally, each domino knocks over the one next to it.

12

See for yourself!

1 Build a tower of blocks, one above the other. The middle of each block is supported by the blocks below. How tall can you make the tower?

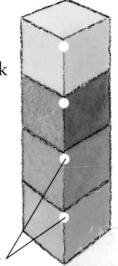

Centres of gravity are above each other.

2 Now try to build a leaning tower, with each block sticking out further than the one below. How tall can you make this tower?

Centre of gravity is not supported.

3 Blocks can help each other balance, if you put them in the right place.

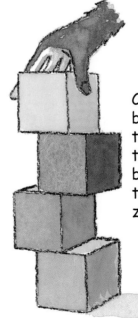

Can you build a taller tower by making the blocks zigzag?

A pyramid is no pushover!

The pyramids built by the Ancient Egyptians have lasted longer than many newer towers. This is because a pyramid is a very stable shape. It is wide at the base and narrow at the top. It has a low centre of gravity and is always supported by its base. With high centres of gravity and narrow bases, towers are more easily toppled by earthquakes and storms.

Pyramid

Collapsing tower

You can't push wobbly toys over!

13

Why does clay change shape?

It's fun making things out of modelling clay or play dough. Like the rest of your toys, clay is solid. It will not run onto the floor, like a liquid, or disappear into the air, like a *gas*. If you do not touch it, clay will stay the same shape. But it is soft, so you can change its shape easily by pushing it in and pulling it out. It will stay in its new shape – until you decide to change it again!

Why did the clay change shape?

It wanted to be a model!

See for yourself!

1 To make play dough, mix a cup of flour, half a cup of salt and a quarter of a cup of water in a bowl. If the mixture is too floury, add more water. If it is too sticky, add more flour.

Salt

Flour

Water

Rolling pin

2 Tip the mixture onto a wooden board and squeeze it with your hands. Roll it out and use biscuit cutters to make different shapes.

Wooden board

Biscuit cutter

14

What is clay?

Natural clay comes from the ground. It has been used for thousands of years to make useful things like bowls, jars and bricks.

You can bend or dent clay, roll it up or flatten it, using either your hands or tools. Shaping clay is called moulding.

Wet clay contains liquid, in which the solid clay *particles* can easily slide to new positions. This is why clay changes shape.

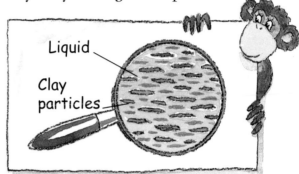

Liquid

Clay particles

If the liquid is removed, by drying, the solid particles in clay can no longer slide around. The clay cannot change shape any more.

Clay can be baked hard in a hot oven called a kiln.

Drying rack

China tea party

WOW!

Very fine white clay is used to make *china*. In the past, some dolls used to be made with china heads, hands and feet.

China dolls

China tea set

A plastic bag will keep your dough soft.

Can my eyes play tricks?

Have you ever wondered how you see things? Light goes through the front of your eye, to make a picture on the *retina* at the back. The retina sends messages to your *brain*, which works out what you are seeing. Your brain has already learnt lots of different pictures. When you see something new, your brain tries to match what it sees to the images it knows. Sometimes, your brain makes mistakes, and your eyes can play tricks on you.

Large or small?

Your brain learns that, when things are far away, they look smaller than when they are near to you. Our eyes can be tricked to think something is large and far away when really it is small and near.

Could these trees be the same size?

Does Marie really have two tails?

Mirror

Reflections can play tricks on you too. They can make things look different or in the wrong place. Sometimes, we think there is more of something than there really is.

See for yourself! ✋

1 Sometimes your eyes see something that can have more than one meaning. Your brain does its best to tell what you are looking at.

Is this an old lady or a girl with a ribbon around her neck?

2 To make a simple kaleidoscope, find two small mirrors that are the same size. Ask an adult to help you tape them firmly together. Stand the mirrors up.

3 Draw a crocodile head. Put your mirrors on part of the picture and look at the reflections. By putting the mirrors in the right place, you can turn it into a flower.

Simple kaleidoscope

Seeing is believing!

WOW!

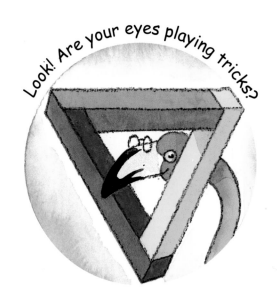

A blind person might recognize an elephant by feeling its trunk, but he or she wouldn't know what it looked like. If that person had their sight restored, their brain would have to learn the 'picture' as an elephant.

Look! Are your eyes playing tricks?

17

What makes toys go?

Toys need *energy* to make them go. When you push or pull them along, muscles in your arm turn *stored energy* into *moving energy*, which is passed on to the toys. Toys that move without you touching them get their energy from elsewhere. Some toys get energy from the wind, others plug into mains *electricity*. But most toys store energy in a *spring* or *battery*. When you switch them on, the stored energy turns into movement, sound and light.

You're winding me up!

What did the toy say to the key?

Energy stores

A clockwork toy has a spring. When you wind it up with a key, your muscles put energy into it. The stored energy is turned into moving energy when you let go of the key.

Key

A wound spring stores energy.

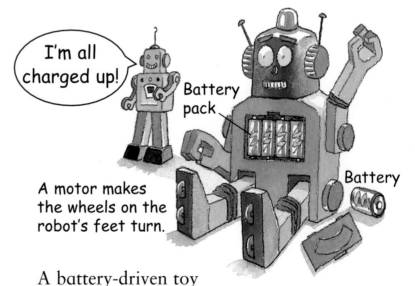

I'm all charged up!

Battery pack

Battery

A motor makes the wheels on the robot's feet turn.

A battery-driven toy carries its own stored energy. When it is switched on, the battery turns energy stored in chemicals into electricity. A *motor* turns this electricity into movement.

See for yourself! ✋

1 To make a windmill, take a square of thin card 10cm by 10cm. Make a hole in the centre and near each corner. Cut a 5cm slit, 2.5cm from each left-hand edge.

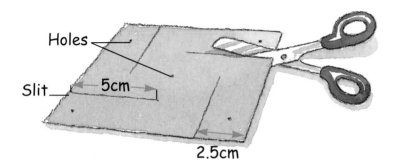

Holes

Slit

5cm

2.5cm

2 Straighten one end of a small paper clip and thread it on a bead. Now bring a corner of the square into the card's centre.

Paper clip

Bead

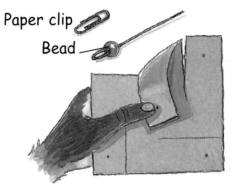

3 Bring the other three corners into the centre. Thread the wire through the holes, and secure it with another bead.

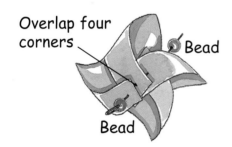

Overlap four corners

Bead

Bead

4 Now twist the wire round a small stick, and hold it in place with sticky tape. Make the windmill spin by blowing on it or holding it in the wind.

Wire

Tape

Stick

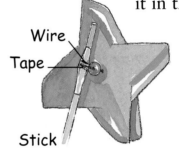

Remote control

WOW!

Toys last longer if you are careful with them.

When you use a remote control toy, the handset sends radio signals to the toy to make it move. The handset and the toy are powered by batteries. Different signals may make the toy go faster or slower, and turn left or right.

How do magnets work?

There are *magnets* in your toys and in many objects around the house. They keep your fridge door closed and stick notes onto it. They also help to pick up pins and needles, and they are even at work inside your TV and loudspeakers. Magnets only attract objects made from certain kinds of metal. The most common of these are iron and steel. The pull, or force, between the magnet and the things it attracts is called *magnetic force*.

You're very forceful!

What did the small magnet say to the big magnet?

Magnetic power

When a magnet moves, it comes to rest with one end (pole) pointing towards Earth's north. This end is north-seeking (N) and the other end of the magnet is south-seeking (S).

Thread

Magnetic North Pole

N

S — Magnet

The Earth is like a giant magnet. The north-seeking pole of the magnet points towards the Earth's North Pole.

The needle in a compass is actually a tiny magnet. One end always points northwards. This helps us find our way.

North

West

East

South

A compass

When something containing iron sticks to a magnet, it becomes a magnet too.

N

North pole

North pole

You can make several paper clips hang from the same magnet.

See for yourself!

1 Put a fridge magnet, or paper clip, on top of a cereal box and hold a strong magnet underneath. Whenever you move the magnet inside the box, the fridge magnet on top follows it.

Strong magnet

2 Now try using a small copper coin. It won't work, because copper is not magnetic, unlike iron or steel.

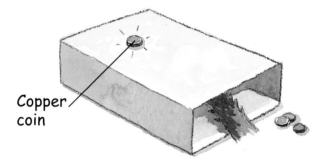

Copper coin

3 To make a theatre, make some scenery to stand behind your box. Draw a figure, such as a ghost, on folded paper and tape a paper clip to its base. You now have a little puppet to glide over your stage.

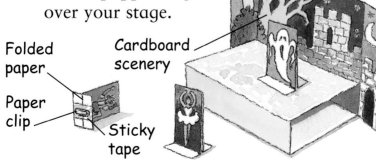

Folded paper

Cardboard scenery

Paper clip

Sticky tape

A rocky compass!

WOW!

North

Some rocks that contain iron also act as magnets. One of these, called lodestone, was used as a compass in Ancient China. Magnets are named after Magnesia, a place in Ancient Greece where lodestone was first found.

Never hold a magnet too close to your TV or video!

21

How does my crane work?

Gravity pulls things towards the ground, so they don't float off into space. Gravity also gives things their *weight* and makes them either heavy or light. In order to lift something up, we have to use a force that pulls against gravity. *Machines* make our work easier. A crane is a machine which helps us to lift and move very heavy objects that we can't lift by hand. It has pulleys to help it do this.

Lifting loads

The longer the pull, the easier it is to lift a load.

Pull

A pulley is a wheel with a rope around its edge. By pulling down on the rope, the load lifts. It is easier to pull downwards than to lift upwards.

A crane can lift a heavy load and put it down somewhere else. When you wind the rope at one end, it lifts the load at the other.

Pulley

Rope

Hook

Handle

Load

22

See for yourself!

1 Thread a shoelace through a short piece of straw and put the straw through the middle of a cotton reel. Tie it to the rung under a chair.

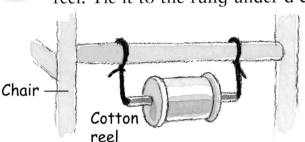

Chair

Cotton reel

2 Thread another reel and tie it firmly round a plastic tub. Put two building blocks in the tub and put it underneath the chair.

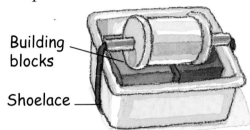

Building blocks

Shoelace

3 Stick one end of a long strip of paper to the top reel with tape. Slip the other end under the lower reel and up and over the top one. Pull gently. The tub will lift easily.

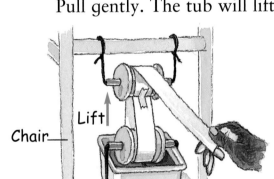

Lift

Chair

4 Now unstick the paper. Fix one end to the lower reel, pass the other end over the top reel and pull. Do you have to pull harder than before to lift the tub?

Lift

A newton of apple!

WOW!

In 1665, Sir Isaac Newton discovered gravity when an apple fell on his head. Force or weight can be measured in newtons. By chance, an apple weighs about one newton.

The load must be lighter than the crane!

How do wheels work?

(speech bubble) What do you call a broken go-cart?

(speech bubble) A stop-cart!

Awheel is round, and it turns on an *axle* going through its centre. Wheels help things move over dry land. A sledge has runners instead of wheels and will slide over snow or wet mud. But it does not run easily over rough ground. Bumps and stones catch on the bottom and cause *friction*, which slows the sledge down. A wheel uses friction to help it turn and move along. The ridges on a *tyre* around the rim help it grip the ground.

Going smoothly

Friction stops things from sliding, but it also helps wheels move. The lowest part of the tyre grips the ground, then lifts off as the next part comes around.

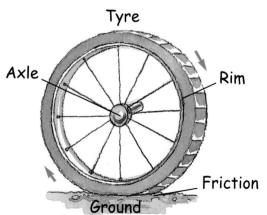

Tyre

Axle

Rim

Friction

Ground

You get a bumpy ride if the axle does not go through the middle of the wheel. This is because, when the wheel turns, the axle moves up and down.

Ball-bearings

Ball-bearings are small steel balls. They are usually found in a ring around axles to help wheels turn smoothly.

24

See for yourself! ✋

1 To make a model car, you will need two small matchbox covers. Cut notches at the end of one. Then cut and fold under half the top at the other end. Do the same with the second cover.

Notches

Cut here

Fold under

2 Slide both covers onto one matchbox drawer. Stick a strip of paper round the boxes to secure them. Give your model a push. It slides like a sledge, but not very far.

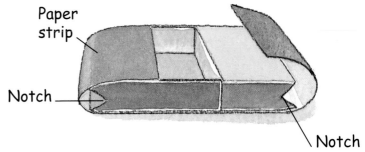

Paper strip

Notch

Notch

3 Cut two pieces of plastic drinking straw and put them through the notches at the ends of your model. These will be axles for your wheels.

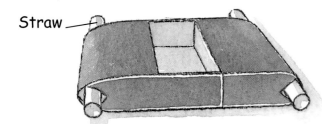

Straw

4 Push four buttons with loops into the ends of the straws. Give your model another push. With its wheels, it will go further and faster.

Button

WOW! Rock and roll!

Stone block

Sledge

Tree trunk rollers

Before the wheel was invented, builders used sledges to move large stone blocks. Tree trunks were used as rollers to reduce friction.

Brakes use friction to stop your bike!

What makes my top spin?

What did the top say to the racing car?

Let's go for a spin!

Have you ever made a toy windmill spin around by blowing on it, or watched a yo-yo spin as its string winds and unwinds? A wheel spins when a motor turns the axle, or when you push the rim along the ground. A spinning top is like a wheel turned on its side. Its axle is vertical, so its rim does not touch anything. You make a top spin by moving the handle quickly, which turns the axle. The faster you make the top spin, the longer it stays up.

How a top stays up

A top falls over when it is not spinning because its weight, acting through its centre of gravity, is high up, and its base is too narrow to support it.

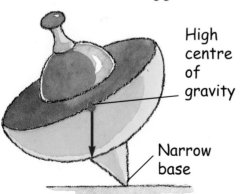

High centre of gravity

Narrow base

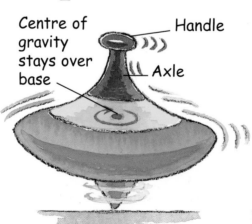

Centre of gravity stays over base

Handle

Axle

While a top is spinning, it moves, so that its weight is always over its base and it cannot fall.

A humming top makes a sound because it has holes which make the air around it *vibrate*.

Air hole

See for yourself! ✋

1 To make a spinner that whistles like a humming top, draw round a saucer on a piece of card and cut out the circle.

Card

Saucer

Scissors

2 Use a hole punch to cut a ring of holes around the circle. Make two more holes in the centre and thread through a long piece of string.

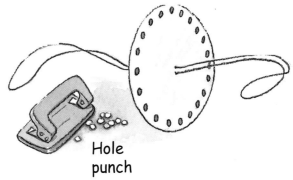

Hole punch

3 Twist the string by swinging the spinner round about 20 times. Pull the string tight, release it, and then pull again. The spinner will whiz round and whistle.

The spinner should be in the middle of the string.

4 Make a spinning top by pushing a pencil stub through a small disc of card. To make it spin, twist the pencil as you drop it onto a smooth surface.

Use coloured pencils to decorate your spinner.

WOW! Perfect balance!

A gyroscope is a heavy spinning top that was invented in 1852 by the French scientist Jean Foucault. When spinning, it is very stable. It stays pointing in whatever direction it is put, so it can be used like a compass on ships and planes.

Look out for other things that spin!

Which toys make noise?

Noisy toys are fun! Rattles, toy trumpets and drums have something in common. When you play or shake them, they squash and stretch the air around them, making it move backwards and forwards. This makes vibrations that reach our ears as sound. If a vibration is trapped inside a space it gets stronger – it *resonates* – and the sound we hear gets louder. Musical instruments are shaped to let this happen.

Which is the noisiest pet?

A trum-pet!

Something in the air

Percussion instruments, such as xylophones and maracas, are shaken or hit to make them vibrate.

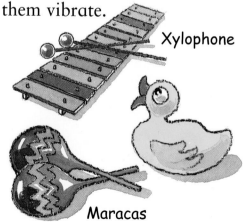

Xylophone

Maracas

Strings

Air vibrates when the strings on a guitar are plucked. The large body of the guitar has space for the air to resonate.

A motor makes this toy car vibrate.

Any toy made of material that will vibrate can make a noise. Moving parts inside toys can cause noisy vibrations.

See for yourself! ✋

1 Although you can't see air vibrating, you can hear it! Collect a selection of drinks bottles and partly fill them with water.

Fill bottles to different levels

2 Now blow across the top of one of the bottles. With a little practice, it will play a note. By holding it when it is resonating, you can feel the whole bottle vibrate.

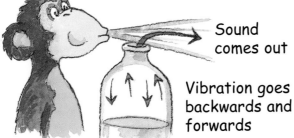

Sound comes out

Vibration goes backwards and forwards

3 To 'retune' a bottle, add more water or tip some out. Arrange the bottles in a row to make a bottle organ.

Too soft for sound

WOW!

Soft, rough surfaces absorb sound energy and cut out resonance. Carpets, curtains, wallpaper and furniture all make your playroom a quieter place.

Empty rooms have an echo.

Toy quiz

1 What colour light does red paint reflect?
a) Red
b) Blue
c) Black

2 What do we call an object that topples over easily?
a) Stable
b) Strong
c) Unstable

3 What happens to clay when it dries?
a) It gets softer
b) It gets harder
c) It turns into a gas

4 In which part of your body is your retina?
a) Your ear
b) Your foot
c) Your eye

5 Where does a clockwork toy get the power to move?
a) From a battery
b) From the Sun
c) From a spring

6 What kind of metal do magnets usually attract?
a) Silver
b) Gold
c) Iron

7 What do you use to lift something off the ground?
a) Friction
b) Force
c) Pressure

8 Where is the axle of a wheel?
a) At the centre
b) Around the edge
c) Between the centre and edge

9 What is a gyroscope?
a) A heavy spinning top
b) A kind of roller-skate
c) A musical instrument

10 What happens to a vibration trapped in a space?
a) It gets stronger
b) It gets weaker
c) It stays the same

Answers on page 32

Glossary

Absorbed
When light is taken in and not released.

Axle
The rod on which a wheel turns.

Battery
An object containing chemicals that store energy. The energy can be released as electricity.

Brain
The part of the body inside the head that receives information and tells the rest of the body what to do.

Centre of gravity
The part of an object where gravity is strongest.

China
Very fine pottery that is made from baked clay.

Electricity
A type of energy carried by a conductor, such as a metal wire.

Energy
The ability to do work or take action.

Force
A push or pull which can change something's movement or shape.

Friction
The force that tries to stop two surfaces from sliding over each other.

Gas
Something like air which has no fixed size or shape and spreads out to fill the space it is in.

Gravity
Earth's downward pull, which makes things fall.

Machines
Structures or objects used to increase force and make work easier.

Magnetic force
The pull between magnets and the metal they attract.

Magnets
Special pieces of metal that attract objects containing iron or steel.

Mass-produced
Made in large numbers, usually by machines.

Motor
A machine that changes electrical or chemical energy into moving energy.

Moulded
When the shape of a soft material is changed by a force on it.

Moving energy
The energy that an object has because it is moving.

Particles
Very small parts of something.

Percussion instruments
Musical instruments that make a noise when they are hit or shaken.

Pigment
A substance used for colouring.

Plastic
Man-made, solid material, made from oil, which can be coloured and moulded into many shapes when hot.

Primary colours
The colours (of pigments or light) that can be mixed together to make all other colours.

Reflected
When light, or sound, is bounced off a surface.

Resonates
Vibrates in such a way that the vibrations get stronger.

Retina
The layer at the back of the eye that sends messages to the brain when light falls on it.

Spring
A coiled piece of metal that stores energy when it is wound up, squashed or stretched.

Stored energy
Energy that is contained in things (like a battery). Stored energy can be converted into other forms of energy.

Tyre
A solid band or air-filled, rubber tube around a wheel's rim, that helps it grip the ground.

Unstable
When something moves out of position easily.

Vertical
Completely upright, straight up and down.

Vibrate
To move backwards and forwards quickly.

Weight
How heavy something is, because of the effects of gravity.

Index

Answers to Toy quiz on page 30
1 Red. **2** Unstable. **3** It gets harder. **4** Your eye.
5 From a spring. **6** Iron. **7** Force. **8** At the centre.
9 A heavy spinning top. **10** It gets stronger.